Mack

# *Whoops!*

## Jonah 1, 2, 3:1–3
### (Jonah and the Fish)

## by Mary Manz Simon
## Illustrated by Dennis Jones

CPH
Concordia Publishing House

## Books by Mary Manz Simon from Concordia Publishing House

### Hear Me Read Level 1 Series
What Next?
Drip Drop
Jibber Jabber
Hide the Baby
Toot! Toot!
Bing!
Whoops!
Send a Baby
A Silent Night
Follow That Star
Row the Boat
Rumble, Rumble
Who Will Help?
Sit Down
Come to Jesus
Too Tall, Too Small
Hurry, Hurry!
Where Is Jesus?

### Hear Me Read Big Book Series
Drip Drop
Who Will Help?
Sit Down
Where Is Jesus?

### Hear Me Read Level 2 Series
The No-Go King
Hurray for the Lord's Army
The Hide-and-Seek Prince
Daniel and the Tattletales
The First Christmas
Through the Roof
A Walk on the Waves
Thank You, Jesus

### Little Visits ® Series
Little Visits on the Go
Little Visits for Toddlers
Little Visits with Jesus
Little Visits Every Day

Stop! It's Christmas
God's Children Pray
My First Diary

5   6   7   8   9   10   11   12   03   02   01   00   99   98

Name

Date

Presented by

**To the Adult:**

Early readers need two kinds of reading. They need to be read to, and they need to do their own reading. The Hear Me Read Bible Stories series helps you to encourage your child with both kinds.

For example, your child might read this book as you sit together. Listen attentively. Assist gently, if needed. Encourage, be patient, and be very positive about your child's efforts.

Then perhaps you'd like to share the selected Bible story in an easy-to-understand translation or paraphrase.

Using both types of reading gives your child a chance to develop new skills and pride in reading. You share and support your child's excitement.

As a mother and a teacher, I anticipate the joy your child will feel in saying, "Hear me read Bible stories!"

*Mary Manz Simon*

**For Matthew**
*Luke 18:16*

"Go," said God.

"Go to the city.

Go to the city now."

"Tell the people about Me," said God.

"Tell the people I am God."

"I do not want to go," said Jonah.

"I do not want to go to the city."

"I will not go to the city," said Jonah.

"I will not go to the city now."

"I will go away from God,"
said Jonah.

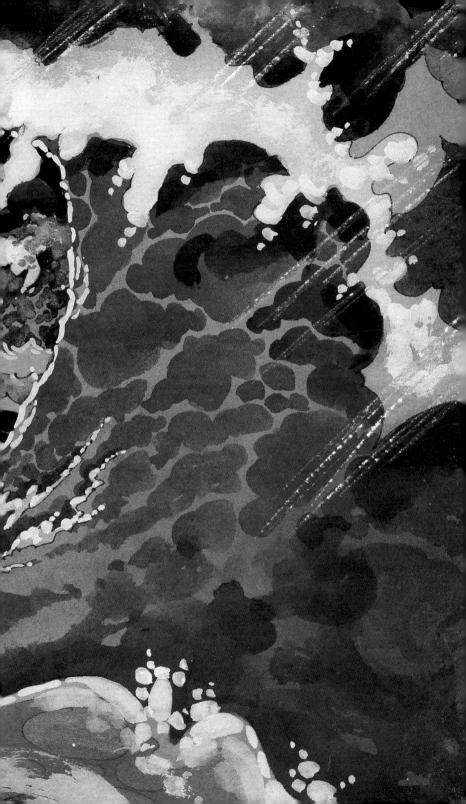

Whoops!

"I did not want to go to the city,"
said Jonah.
"I wanted to go away from God."

"Now I am sorry," said Jonah.

"I am sorry I wanted to

go away from God.

I am sorry I did not

go to the city."

Whoops!

"Go," said God.

"Go to the city.

Go to the city now."

"Tell the people about Me,"
God said.
"Tell the people I am God."

"I will go," said Jonah.
"I will go now."

"I will go to the city," said Jonah.
"I will tell the people
about God."

## About the Author

Mary Manz Simon holds a doctoral degree in education with a specialty in early childhood education. She has taught at levels from preschool through postgraduate. Dr. Simon is the bestselling author of more than 30 children's books, including *Little Visits with Jesus*. She and her husband, the Reverend Henry A. Simon, are the parents of three children.